LAKE DISTRICT DISCOVERY GUIDES

North Lakes

View from Low Fell over the Lorton valley and Crummock Water

ROBERT GRANGE

BUTTERMERE AND CRUMMOCK

The beautiful horseshoe-shaped Buttermere valley contains both Buttermere and Crummock Water. The village of Buttermere lies between the two stretches of water and can be reached by the famous Honister Pass linking the valley with Keswick

This commanding panoramic view is taken from Rannerdale Knotts, high above the eastern shores of Crummock Water; the village of Buttermere nestles in the trees in front of the lake beyond. The fells of the surrounding valley were among the favourite walks of the late Alfred Wainwright, the author of the classic walking guides to the Lake District, and have been immortalised in his guidebooks. The walk known as the Buttermere Horseshoe starts on Red Pike on the right, and then runs onto High Stile and Haystacks. Great Gable is hiding in the distance. The ridge of Fleetwith Pike stands proud at the entrance to Honister Pass. Robinson completes the picture on the left, hiding in the shade of Buttermere Moss.

MELBREAK

As you head north-west out of Buttermere village towards Cockermouth you will quickly catch sight of the steep-sided fell of Melbreak which rises abruptly above the far shore of Crummock Water to your left. The annual fell race takes runners to the twin peaks of this formidable fell

High above Crummock Water on its western shore is Melbreak, a stunning fell with near sheer cliffs plunging into the deep blue waters of the lake. It is a much-loved hill for its ever changing texture and wide range of colours throughout the seasons. Its sides are carved with deep gullies and barren screes that work their way through the fields of heather. It has to be one of the quietest hills in the Lake District – in fact, it is rare to see another walker. This could be due to its position on the edge of the Lakes or the fact that you have to undertake a lengthy walk for the satisfaction of climbing just one peak.

FLEETWITH

The highly photogenic Fleetwith Pike sits proudly at the southern end of Buttermere. From its summit, there is a spectacular view back down the Buttermere Valley. Dubbs Hut, a boathouse, is a focal point for walkers and tourists

Standing proud in the Buttermere valley, a brooding presence above the lake, is Fleetwith Pike. Its impressive nose is reflected in the mirror calm waters of Buttermere along with the snow-covered grey crags of Brandreth on the right above Dubbs Hut and Warnscale Bottom.

STORM BREWING

The westerly-facing Lake District is famous for prolonged and often unexpected bouts of heavy rain. Wet weather is not popular with tourists but it adds an extra dimension to the spectacular beauty of the region

Of the many sports and pastimes undertaken in the national park, one of the most popular is fishing. With their early starts and remote locations they are often missed by the ever present rambler, but if you look you will nearly always find a fisherman on the shores of a lake or on the banks of one of the many rivers. Here in the waters of Buttermere, with a storm brewing over Fleetwith Pike and Haystacks, a fisherman casts a fly to the feeding fish.

Scale Force, which Wordsworth described as a 'fine chasm, with a lofty, though slender, fall of water', is the largest waterfall in the Lake District. The fast-flowing Scale Beck tumbles down the steep slopes of Red Pike into the Buttermere valley. But at this point, it disappears into a crevice in the rock and the water is forced to freefall over 100ft (30.5m) down a narrow chasm making it the tallest waterfall in England. It was a wet day when this photograph was taken and the stream was high, but that was nothing compared to the force of water that must have been needed to move the trees and boulders in the stream bed. It would be wonderful to see the waterfall in full flow, but not from the spot where this photograph was taken!

There are scenes of outstanding natural beauty to be found every day in the Lake District. Even when it is pouring with rain and the hills are shrouded in cloud, the waterfalls are impressive. The way the water bumbles its way downstream, bumping into rocks and boulders, is fascinating. This photograph, which attempts to convey the mesmerising motion of the water and the mood of the stream, was taken on a slow shutter speed. The first of the autumn leaves falling on the rocks and water adds the final touch to this view of Lodore Falls in Borrowdale, formed by water from Watendlath Tarn cascading over huge boulders.

BORROWDALE

Considered by many to be the most beautiful valley in England,
Borrowdale lies at the southern end of Derwent Water

Upper Borrowdale was carved out millennia ago by glaciers. Here, you are looking south in the morning sun. The early summer greens of the bracken and trees stand out in the sharp light. At the bottom of the frame you can see the river Derwent and Stonethwaite Beck. Follow the line up the valley and you come to the villages of Rosthwaite and Stonethwaite. The backdrop of mountains from left to right includes Harrison Stickle on the edge of the Langdales, Glaramara, then on to Great End, which is just playing in cloud, and finally Great Gable on the right.

For those of you who think you have walked all the best Lakeland fells, here is a view to be reckoned with. High above the village of Grange is King's How, a short but steep walk from the village. It gives a viewpoint unsurpassed in the valley with Skiddaw and Derwent Water to the north, Catbells on the left and Surprise View on the right.

The river Derwent starts its circuitous journey in Borrowdale and flows through two lakes (Derwent Water and Bassenthwaite Lake) before making its way into the Irish Sea close to Workington. In its upper reaches – the Derwent is seen here between Borrowdale and Derwent Water just below Shepherd's Crag – the river is so wide and slow-moving that it's easy to mistake it for one of the many lakes in this part of the world.

DERWENT WATER

Derwent Water has a magnificent setting. To the west lie the fells of Catbells and High Spy ridge; to the north the dramatic peaks of Skiddaw, Hindscarth, High Stile and Causey Pike

The east and southern lakeside also have their fair share of dramatic scenery from the Central Fells to Borrowdale and the lakeside here is covered in beautiful woodland that is a delight for walkers. Despite the close proximity of Keswick, which lies on the north-eastern edge of Derwent Water, the area boasts many quiet and beautiful spots which have helped to earn this stretch of water the well-deserved title 'Queen of the Lakes'.

Even after many years in the Lake District there are certain views that can leave one lost for words. On this particular evening there was a high level of cirrus, wispy, white ice cloud which heralded a band of bad weather. The setting sun caught this, leaving the sky gorgeous shades of purple and pink.

CATBELLS

A trip on the lake, whether it's on a cruiser or rowing boat, is a 'must' for any visitor to Derwent Water. One of the most recognisable ridges on the far side of the water from Keswick is the dome-shaped Catbells

As the mist lifts, it leaves a placid scene. The distant peak of Catbells is reflected in the calm of Derwent Water – a great location for an early morning paddle. The only noise that can be heard is the water running against the boat and the slurp of the paddle in the water.

Throughout autumn, as the nights cool down, the morning often starts with a carpet of mist covering the valley floors. This is one of the season's most stunning sights, but you need to climb the hills before dawn to appreciate the view. As the sun gathers warmth, the mist slowly breaks and rises, making patterns like tufts of cottonwool in the middle of the valley. Looking from Surprise View in Borrowdale, down onto Derwent Water and Manesty, the wisps are just catching a little of the dawn light.

SKIDDAW

Skiddaw dominates the skyline just north of Keswick. Its distinctive triangular shape, with a number of lower peaks, make it one of the most easily identified mountains in the north lakes

With clouds above and clouds below, Skiddaw (3053ft/931m) is in view for most of the walk around Derwent Water. Here, the mist still hangs in the valley and the first clouds of the day are on the hills. This stunning image is perfectly mirrored in the lake.

SKIDDAW FROM CATBELLS

Catbells offers one of the most dramatic views in all of the North Lakes. From the summit you overlook the Skiddaw Massif to the north, the busy town of Keswick to the north-east and, looking down Derwent Water to the south, the dramatic 'jaws of Borrowdale'

A crisp clear morning on the summit of Catbells offers a wonderful view of the vale of Keswick and the Newlands Valley. This has to be the north Lakes' most popular walk, and on many summer days there is a constant line of people on the ridge from morning till evening. With a view like this you can see why: on the left there is Bassenthwaite Lake and the Skiddaw massif overlooking the wooded hill of Swinside at the foot of Catbells. Rising from the silvery lake is the last of the morning mist.

A 'family-friendly' fellside, Catbells is a favourite with walkers. The path winds its way through the grassy hillside to a rockier summit. The more adventurous walker can continue on to Maiden Moor and High Spy. And if you've still got the energy you can keep going until you reach Robinson (seen here on the right of the photograph).

KESWICK AND SKIDDAW

Wander a few minutes off the beaten track and away from the busy streets of Keswick and the visitor will be rewarded by easily accessible and dramatic views over the surrounding countryside

Above the little bridge at Ashness and through the trees there is a small car park. Just a few steps leads you to Surprise View, a beauty spot overlooking Derwent Water, Keswick and Skiddaw which has a wonderful view on almost any day. Here, the small oak trees that line the steep valley sides have changed to a brilliant orange with the first of the winter's frosts.

With most visitors coming to the Lake District in the summer few get to see the snow-capped peaks of winter. A dusting of snow gives extra drama to the hills, a greater sense of their height and mystery. There again, the excitement at seeing the snow on the hills is often a reaction to weeks of grey driving rain.

CASTLERIGG

The Castlerigg Stone Circle, one and a half miles east of Keswick, is guaranteed to inspire visitors. One hundred feet in diameter, it is set in an open common amidst a bowl of surrounding fells. This mysterious monument is seen at its breathtaking best at dawn or dusk

Castlerigg dawn
The dawn is one of the most mysterious times of the day. Here the sun is slowly rising over Threlkeld Common, lighting the standing stones of Castlerigg at the beginning of another day. Known locally as 'Druid's Circle', the exact function of the Castlerigg stones is shrouded in mystery. Like Stonehenge, the circle has its own summer solstice celebrations when crowds gather to watch the sun rise slowly over the stones.

Castlerigg at sunset
This mysterious stone circle, which consists of 38 stones, has stood for thousands of years on the brow of Castlerigg. Many people believe it to have been a trading point for Langdale axes, while others think that the silhouette of the stones marks the changing of the seasons. The awe-inspiring view in this photograph was captured during a wild sunset at the end of a stormy autumn day.

Ashness Bridge
The small packhorse bridge over Ashness Gill has to be one of the most famous bridges in England. It was first brought into the photographic hall of fame by the Abraham Brothers of Keswick at the turn of the century. It benefits from the wonderful backdrop of Derwent Water and Skiddaw. Although the lake can be seen here, many trees have grown up in the last 100 years and the view is quiet different from the one captured by the brothers all those years ago.

Great Gable and its sister peak Green Gable lie
in the wild and desolate country between
Buttermere and Wast Water. Seen from Wasdale,
Great Gable is of perfectly rounded proportions –
which is why it was chosen as the central motif
of the Lake District National Park

Great and Green Gable stand proud, nestling into each
other with a wind gap, the coll, between. Patchy snow
highlights the rugged boulder-strewn landscape that makes
the heart of the Lake District such a barren yet beautiful
wilderness every month of the year. The photograph below
was taken on the same day and shows the daunting snow-
covered ridge of Great Gable in stark outline.

TEWET TARN

Between Threlkeld and Keswick on the A66 just as you pass Clough Head you will spot a small stretch of water known as Tewet Tarn. This little tarn is usually missed by the passing visitor but it offers wonderful views of two of the North Lakes' most dramatic mountains – Skiddaw and Blencathra

These photographs are of a view that is often overlooked. Tewet Tarn sits in the middle of St John's in the Vale and can be missed by both Lake District locals and visitors alike. A farmer dammed it many years ago, little realising that he would create such a wonderful vantage point of the Skiddaw Forest as these two photographs show. On the left Carl Side rises out onto Little Man and then Skiddaw. Lonscale Fell sits alongside. The rugged ridge of Blencathra is shown in the second photograph. Follow the skyline onto Scales Fell to complete the picture.

BLENCATHRA

The approach to Keswick along the A66 is dominated by Blencathra. With its looming presence and plethora of interesting and challenging walks, it is the favourite mountain of many visitors to the Lake District

Blencathra, popularly known as 'Saddleback', towers over the north-eastern corner of the Lake District. At 2847ft (867m) it is the region's second highest peak. Its massive bulk, often the first to be topped by snow in winter, makes it a mountain you simply cannot ignore anywhere in or around Keswick. Here the early winter snowfall adds drama to one of the most popular ascents from the White Horse Inn via Scales Fell and the east ridge. In the summer this route makes for a classic walk but in the winter it should be left to the more hardened mountaineers. On the east side of the mountain is the even more intimidating long narrow ridge known as Sharp Edge, regarded by mountaineers as a classic route to the summit.

This majestic waterfall powers down over 100ft (30.5m) of rock. The rock pools have been carved out over thousands of years by the river Aira and they nestle in the small valley between Gowbarrow and Watermillock Common. Whatever the weather, Aira Force is a very dramatic stopping point for visitors on any tour of the northern Lakes.

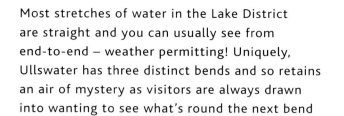

Most stretches of water in the Lake District
are straight and you can usually see from
end-to-end — weather permitting! Uniquely,
Ullswater has three distinct bends and so retains
an air of mystery as visitors are always drawn
into wanting to see what's round the next bend

The early morning has an atmosphere all of its own.
From the shore at Skelly Neb, halfway down the north
side of Ullswater, you can see Howtown on the left
with the dark outline of Hallin Fell and Place Fell in the
distance. The early morning is often the best part of
the day, and this one was no exception. This photograph
was taken at about 7am; cloud was already beginning
to cover the sky and it was raining by noon.

HAWESWATER

Haweswater is the most easterly of the lakes and for the last 70 years has been used as a reservoir to supply Manchester. As the water level of the reservoir drops, the surrounding banks of bleached stones become exposed leaving a deep white fringe all around the edge of the lake.

First published in 2005 by
Myriad Books Limited
35 Bishopsthorpe Road
London SE26 4PA

Photographs copyright © Robert Grange
Text copyright © Robert Grange

Robert Grange has asserted his right under the Copyright, Designs and Patents Act 1998 to be identified as the author of this work.

ISBN 1 904 736 12 2

Designed by Phillip Appleton

Printed in China

www.myriadbooks.com